raw CAKES

30 DELICIOUS, **NO-BAKE, VEGAN, SUGAR-FREE** & **GLUTEN-FREE** CAKES

JOANNA FARROW

spruce

An Hachette UK Company
www.hachette.co.uk

First published in Great Britain in 2016 by Spruce
a division of Octopus Publishing Group Ltd
Carmelite House, 50 Victoria Embankment
London EC4Y 0DZ
www.octopusbooks.co.uk
www.octopusbooksusa.com

Distributed in the US by Hachette Book Group
1290 Avenue of the Americas, 4th and 5th Floors,
New York, NY10020

Distributed in Canada by Canadian Manda Group
664 Annette Street, Toronto, Ontario, Canada M6S 2C8

ISBN: 978-1-84601-526-7

A CIP catalogue record for this book is available from the
British Library

Printed and bound in China

10 9 8 7 6 5 4 3 2 1

Both metric and imperial measurements have
been given in all recipes. Use one set of measurements
only, and not a mixture of both.

Standard level spoon measurements are used in all recipes
1 tablespoon = 15 ml spoon
1 teaspoon = 5 ml spoon

This book includes dishes made with nuts and nut
derivatives. It is advisable for people with known allergic
reactions to nuts and nut derivatives or those who may be
potentially vulnerable to these allergies, such as pregnant
and nursing mothers, invalids, the elderly, babies and
children, to avoid dishes made with these. It is prudent to
check the labels of all pre-prepared ingredients for the
possible inclusion of nut derivatives.

CONTENTS

INTRODUCTION

WHAT IS A RAW FOOD DIET?

In a world that increasingly relies on the convenience of ready-meals, fast food, and a daily latte-to-go, the idea of a raw food diet probably seems like an alien concept to many. And yet, an increasing number of people are turning their backs on mass-produced processed food and discovering the health and lifestyle benefits of raw foods.

Raw food is defined as food that is not cooked at temperatures above 118°F (48°C). Ingredients are generally vegan, organic, unprocessed, and don't contain any wheat, dairy, refined sugar, soy, or yeast. Committed followers of a raw food diet aim to eat at least 75 percent of their food raw, and the diet mainly consists of vegetables, fruits, nuts, sprouts, and seeds.

THE HEALTH BENEFITS

People choose to adopt a raw food diet for many different reasons: concerns about the environment, a desire to maximize vitamin and mineral intake, or to make healthy choices for their family. Whatever the reasons, there are certainly many benefits to introducing raw foods to your diet.

TURN UP THE HEAT

Cooking food at high temperatures destroys many of the enzymes that aid digestion, so it follows that raw food can be more easily digested by the body. By eating raw foods you are harnessing all the nutritional power of each ingredient and you know exactly which vitamins and minerals your body is digesting.

POSITIVE ENERGY

When you conserve the energy in your food, all that energy is passed on to you. Raw foodists claim to feel more energetic and certainly avoid the bloated and lethargic feeling that can often follow a cooked meal.

RAW CAKE INGREDIENTS

The following ingredients are the mainstay of the vegan raw food pantry. Plenty of other dried fruit, nuts, seeds, and grains are also used extensively but those listed below include several you might not be familiar with. All are widely available from supermarkets, health food stores, or online wholefood suppliers. Check all labeling when buying to make sure products are genuinely raw.

Agave nectar Extracted from the agave plant, this syrup is sometimes used as an alternative to regular sugar in raw and cooked dishes. Some types are heat-treated during production so make sure you buy "raw".

Maple syrup Maple syrup is heat-treated during processing but is used in raw cake recipes because it's richer in nutrients than agave nectar and is considered by many raw foodists as an exception to the "raw" rule. It's available in several different grades or strengths. The darker ones are extracted later in the harvesting season and have a richer flavor. Read the label carefully to avoid buying "maple flavor syrup", which might be a regular cane syrup with maple flavoring added.

Coconut palm sugar and blossom nectar Extracted from the coconut palm, the nectar and sugar have a rich, caramel flavor and a higher nutritional content than other forms of sweetener. They are also lower on the Glycemic Index (GI) than maple, agave, and cane sugars.

Dates Naturally sweet and toffee-like in consistency, dates are a staple of raw cake recipes. Types such as Medjool, Deglet Nour, and Halawi are popular, though prices vary and they might be soft and plump or firmer and chewy. Try several varieties to see which you like best; it's a matter of taste. If using a firm variety, chop them first so they are easier to blend to a paste.

Cacao butter

Cacao butter is the creamy-colored, edible fat extracted from the cacao bean. Unlike the name suggests, it is extremely hard and must be chopped and melted before it can be used in raw cakes. Using a cutting board and sturdy, sharp knife, chop the cacao butter into small pieces; some will break into slivers, but simply tip the lot into a small heatproof bowl to melt (see Techniques for details). Cacao butter solidifies on cooling, making it useful for thickening and binding together other raw cake ingredients.

Cacao powder Raw cacao powder is ground from unroasted cacao beans and is a highly nutritious food, renowned for its antioxidant power. Unlike regular cocoa powder, raw cacao powder is not heat-treated during production and hence retains its vital nutrients. Used to flavor fillings and toppings, it has a rich, bitter chocolate taste that requires sweetening or combining with a naturally sweet, dried fruit paste or puree.

Coconut oil Coconut oil is opaque and solid, even at room temperature. After melting for use in raw cakes (see Techniques) it returns to its set form, making it useful for thickening and binding together fillings and toppings for raw cakes.

TECHNIQUES

Raw cakes are easy to make and benefit from the fact that there's no cooking and cooling involved to prolong preparation time. The following simple techniques are used frequently in the recipes.

MELTING

Coconut oil and cacao butter both need melting before use. Coconut oil has a buttery, set consistency at room temperature that melts very easily. Cacao butter is very solid and takes longer to melt to a usable, liquid form. To speed up melting and avoid the risk of overheating it, chop cacao butter first (see above).

Put the measured amount of oil or butter in a small, heatproof bowl. Pour a little boiling water into a larger heatproof bowl and lower the smaller bowl into it. Let stand until melted, stirring occasionally. If the boiling water has cooled before the butter or oil has melted, replace with more boiled water. This occasionally happens when melting a large amount of cacao butter.

SOAKING NUTS

Before use, all nuts must be soaked in water for several hours, or overnight if you think sufficiently ahead. Harder nuts like almonds need longer soaking than softer ones such as cashews. If you're short of time, soaking nuts for an hour or so is better than not soaking them at all. Soaking improves nuts' digestibility and increases the absorption of the nutrients they provide into the body. For walnuts, it also reduces the bitter flavor, which can be very harsh. Simply put the nuts in a bowl and cover with plenty of cold water. Always discard the water after soaking. If using the nuts in cookies or firmer cakes, pat them dry after draining to remove the excess moisture.

SCRAPING DOWN MIXTURES FROM PROCESSOR BOWLS
During processing, pieces of fruit, nuts, and other ingredients can cling to the sides of the processor bowl. For evenly blended mixtures, scrape the ingredients down from the sides of the bowl at frequent intervals with a plastic spatula.

GETTING THE RIGHT CONSISTENCY
For cheesecake and tart crusts, bars, and some cake crusts, the ingredients need to be blended in the processor to a point where they start to cling together. This ensures that the mixture will pack down firmly and/or hold together once transferred to the pan. It'll also make it easier to cut. When the ingredients are finely chopped, stop the machine and pinch a little mixture between your thumb and finger. If it holds together it's ready to use. If still very crumbly, process it for a little longer.

LINING PANS
Most of the recipes recommend pans. These can be metal baking pans or any other container you have of similar dimensions. Line with a sheet of plastic wrap or parchment paper, pushing the lining right into the corners before smoothing or creasing it up the sides. Dampening the pan or container with a little water first will help keep plastic wrap in place.

PRESSING CAKE MIXTURES INTO PANS
Packing the mixture down in the pan creates a firm texture that makes cutting the cake easier. This is particularly important for cheesecake crusts, pies, and bars. Tip the mixture into the pan and spread out in an even layer. Press down firmly with the back of a spoon or your fingertips. It's best to do this quickly first and then go over the mixture again. Dampening the the spoon will help prevent the mixture from sticking to it. If the mixture is sticky and clings to the spoon, use a clean spoon. For pie crusts such as Chocolate Mud Pie (see page 32), press the mixture up the sides of the pan before pressing the remainder into the bottom.

REMOVING CAKES FROM LOOSE-BOTTOM PANS
Loose-bottom pans are used for recipes where the top of the cake would be damaged if the cake was inverted out of a pan, such as Raw Banoffi Pie (see page 24). To remove the cake from the pan, rest the bottom of the pan on a small upturned bowl and gently pull the sides of the pan down.

WHIPPING COCONUT CREAM AND COCONUT MILK

Coconut cream and coconut milk can be whipped until softly peaking, making a delicious topping for raw cakes or a perfect accompaniment to cakes you might like to serve as a dessert, such as Coconut Neapolitan Cake (see page 43), Apple and Cardamom Crumble Cakes (see page 14) and Plum and Oatmeal Upside-Down Cake (see page 28). Chill the can of coconut cream or full-fat coconut milk thoroughly first, preferably overnight, so that the contents separate. Spoon the coconut cream or milk out of the can into a bowl, leaving the clear, thin layer of water in the bottom of the can. (With coconut cream there will be very little water left in the can, more so for coconut milk. Keep this for another recipe.) Beat using an electric hand beater

or egg whisk until softly peaking. To serve as an accompaniment, lightly sweeten with a drizzle of maple syrup or agave nectar if you prefer.

STORING RAW CAKES

While some raw cakes, such as the Fruity Breakfast Bars (see page 12), Raw Gingerbread Cookies (see page 16), Chewy Berry Bites (see page 56), Chocolate Orange Nuggets (see page 57), and Almond and Walnut Fudge (see page 61), store well in an airtight container for up to 2 days, most of the cakes in this book are best consumed within 24 hours of making.

EQUIPMENT

If you're already a raw foodist you probably have all the utensils and equipment you need to create the recipes in this book. However, if you're just beginning your raw food culinary journey there are a few essential items that will help ensure you achieve the best results.

Knives Don't scrimp when it comes to knives. Choose a large chopping knife for chopping nuts and dried fruit. A small paring knife and vegetable peeler are handy for fruit and vegetable preparation.

Food processor This is an essential piece of equipment for making raw cakes and is used in most of the recipes. It'll chop, blend, and puree ingredients to a consistency that's almost impossible to achieve by hand. It's worth splashing out on a large, sturdy processor as a cheap one won't grind ingredients smoothly and won't last as long.

Blender There are many powerful juicers, blenders, and smoothie makers now available that are great for raw cake fillings. Although the recipes in this book suggest a food processor, use a powerful blender if you have one for making nut-based fillings as it will blend the mixture until completely smooth, a texture that's not always achievable in a food processor.

Baking pans and dishes For obvious reasons, the choice of pan or dish for your cake is far wider than it would be if baking. Although the recipes usually suggest cake pans, you can use any similar-size container, whether glass, plastic, or any other material.

chocolate mousse cake
WITH SUMMER BERRIES

SERVES 6 • **PREP TIME** 25 minutes plus chilling

2¾ oz (75 g) coconut oil

2 ripe avocados

Scant ½ cup (50 g) cacao powder

Scant ½ cup (100 ml) agave nectar

2 teaspoons vanilla extract

Squeeze of lemon juice

⅓ cup (50 g) raspberries

⅓ cup (50 g) blueberries or halved blackberries

Cut 6 x 6 inch (15 cm) squares of parchment paper. Press a square over an upturned dariole mold, creasing it down the sides to fit. Lift away and push the paper into the mold to form a lining. (Creasing it over the outside of the mold first makes it easier to fit neatly inside.) Repeat to line 5 more molds. Alternatively, line 6 sections of a cupcake pan with paper cupcake cups.

Put the coconut oil in a small heatproof bowl and stand it in a larger heatproof bowl of boiling water. Let melt.

Put the avocados, cacao powder, agave nectar, vanilla extract, and lemon juice in a food processor and process until smooth, scraping down the mixture from the sides of the bowl. Add the melted coconut oil and process again. Spoon the mixture into the prepared molds or cups and chill for several hours or overnight.

Top the cakes with the raspberries and blueberries or blackberries and serve.

salted
PECAN BROWNIES

MAKES 16 • PREP TIME 10 minutes plus soaking

1½ cups (150 g) pecans

2¼ cups (400 g) pitted dates,
 coarsely chopped

Scant ¼ cup (50 ml) maple syrup

Generous ½ cup (65 g) cacao powder

Good pinch of salt

FOR THE TOPPING:

Generous ½ cup (100 g) pitted dates,
 coarsely chopped

½ teaspoon sea salt

1 tablespoon maple syrup

3–4 tablespoons water

Put the pecans in a bowl, cover with cold water and let soak for several hours or overnight.

Line a 6 inch (15 cm) square shallow baking pan or similar-size container with plastic wrap or parchment paper.

Drain the nuts and pat dry with paper towels, then transfer to a food processor and process briefly until chopped. Remove half the nuts and set aside.

Continue to process the remaining nuts until finely ground. Add the dates, maple syrup, cacao powder, and salt and process thoroughly, scraping down the mixture from the sides of the bowl, until it forms a thick paste. Add the reserved chopped nuts and pulse briefly until

combined. Turn the mixture into the prepared pan and press down firmly.

To make the topping, wipe out the processor, add the dates and salt, and process to a paste. Add the maple syrup and enough of the measurement water to form a spreadable paste.

Lift the brownie slab out of the pan and peel away the plastic wrap or paper. Spread over the topping and serve cut into 16 small squares.

FRUITY BREAKFAST BARS

MAKES 16 • PREP TIME 10 minutes plus soaking

⅓ cup (50 g) flax seeds

Scant ¼ cup (50 ml) coconut water

1½ teaspoons pumpkin pie spice

Finely grated zest of 1 orange

1¾ oz (50 g) coconut oil

2½ cups (250 g) rolled oats

Generous ½ cup (100 g) raisins

Generous ¼ cup (40 g) sunflower seeds

⅓ cup (40 g) pumpkin seeds

1 cup (200 g) dried figs, stalks removed

1 cup (100 g) dried banana slices

Scant ½ cup (100 ml) agave nectar

Line a 7 inch (18 cm) square shallow baking pan or similar-size container with plastic wrap or parchment paper. Grind the flax seeds to a powder in a small spice or coffee grinder, or food processor. Tip into a small bowl, add the coconut water, spice, and orange zest, and set aside. Put the coconut oil in a small heatproof bowl and stand it in a larger heatproof bowl of boiling water. Let melt.

Combine the oats, raisins, and seeds in a large bowl. Put the figs and banana slices in a food processor and process to a smooth, thick paste. Add the agave nectar, melted coconut oil, and flax seed mixture and process again until combined. Add the fruit paste to the dry ingredients and mix with a spoon or spatula until thoroughly combined and no dry ingredients remain.

Turn the mixture into the prepared pan and press down firmly. Chill or let stand in a cool place for several hours or overnight until firm. Serve cut into 16 bars.

FRESH GINGER & OAT BARS

MAKES 16 • PREP TIME 10 minutes plus soaking

1¾ cups (300 g) pitted prunes

2 inch (5 cm) piece of fresh ginger root, grated

2½ tablespoons tahini paste

4 tablespoons sesame seeds

½ cup (75 g) medium oatmeal

¾ cup (75 g) buckwheat flakes

Generous ½ cup (100 g) golden raisins

4 tablespoons apple juice

Line a loaf pan with a base measurement of 8½ x 3½ inches (22 x 9 cm), or a similar-size container, with plastic wrap.

Put a scant 1¼ cups (200 g) of the prunes, the ginger, and tahini paste in a food processor and process until smooth, scraping down the mixture from the sides of the bowl. Add 3 tablespoons of the sesame seeds, the oatmeal, and buckwheat and process again until combined. Add the golden raisins and pulse briefly. Turn the mixture into the prepared pan and press down firmly in an even layer.

Wipe out the processor and process the remaining prunes and the apple juice until very smooth. Spread over the filling and sprinkle with the remaining sesame seeds. Lift out of the pan and serve cut into bars.

apple & cardamom
CRUMBLE CAKES

MAKES 6 • PREP TIME 30 minutes plus soaking

⅔ cup (100 g) hazelnuts

¾ cup (75 g) dried apple rings, coarsely chopped

12 cardamom pods

5 red dessert apples

Finely grated zest of 1 lemon, plus 4 teaspoons juice

Generous ½ cup (100 g) golden raisins, chopped

2 tablespoons finely chopped mint, plus extra leaves to decorate

4 teaspoons agave nectar

Put the hazelnuts in a bowl, cover with cold water and let soak for several hours or overnight.

Thoroughly drain the nuts, then transfer to a food processor with the apple rings and process until the mixture is finely chopped and starts to cling together.

Crush the cardamom pods using a mortar and pestle. Scoop out and discard the shells and crush the seeds a little more.

Peel 2 of the apples, or until you have enough peel to make 6 strips, each about 7 inches (18 cm) long. Pour boiling water into a small heatproof bowl, add 1 teaspoon of the lemon juice and the apple strips and let stand for 2 minutes until slightly softened. Rinse in cold water and set aside.

Quarter and core all the apples and grate, including the skin of the unpeeled apples, into a large bowl. Stir in the crushed cardamom, golden raisins, lemon zest and remaining juice, mint, and agave nectar.

Place 6 x 2¾ inch (7 cm) baking rings on a baking sheet. (If you only have one ring, simply shape one at a time. You can also use a metal cookie cutter.) Spoon a third of the nut crumble mixture into the rings and press down firmly. Spoon half the apple mixture on top and press down firmly, making sure the apples are evenly distributed. Pack half the remaining crumble mixture on top, then the remaining apple mixture and finally the rest of the crumble. The cakes can be chilled for several hours or served straight away.

To serve, carefully lift away the metal rings. Roll up each strip of apple peel to resemble a small rose and position on top of the cakes, adding mint leaves to decorate.

raw gingerbread
COOKIES

MAKES 15 • PREP TIME 15 minutes plus soaking and standing

1 cup (100 g) pecans, plus 15 pecan halves to decorate

Generous ½ cup (100 g) raisins

1¼ cups (125 g) rolled oats

4 tablespoons coconut palm sugar

1 teaspoon ground ginger

1 teaspoon pumpkin pie spice

¼ teaspoon ground cloves

Good pinch of hot chili powder

Put the pecans in a bowl, cover with cold water and let soak for several hours or overnight. Drain and pat dry with paper towels.

Transfer the nuts to a food processor, add the raisins and 1 cup (100 g) of the oats, and process until the mixture forms fine crumbs. Add the coconut palm sugar and spices, then process again until the dough starts to clump together. Add the remaining oats and pulse briefly to combine.

Divide the dough into 15 pieces, then shape into balls. Position a 2 inch (5 cm) cookie cutter over a ball on the counter and flatten out the dough to fill the cutter. Lift the cutter away and press a pecan half into the center. Repeat with the remaining balls. Serve immediately or store in an airtight container for several days.

APRICOT & BUTTERNUT CUPCAKES

MAKES 9 • PREP TIME 20 minutes plus overnight soaking, chilling and standing

⅔ cup (100 g) almonds, plus extra
    to decorate

Generous ½ cup (100 g) macadamia nuts

1½ oz (40 g) coconut oil

Generous ½ cup (100 g) plump dried
    apricots

7 oz (200 g) skinned, seeded, and chopped
    butternut squash

1 inch (2.5 cm) piece of fresh ginger root,
    coarsely chopped

⅓ cup (50 g) coconut palm sugar

Maple syrup, to serve (optional)

FOR THE TOPPING:

1 oz (25 g) coconut oil

4 fresh apricots, halved, pitted,
    and quartered

1 (14 oz/400 g) can coconut milk,
    chilled overnight

Put all the nuts in a bowl, cover with cold water and let soak for several hours or overnight. Drain thoroughly.

Place a large sheet of plastic wrap over a 12-section cupcake pan, then press into 9 of the sections to line them.

Put the coconut oil in a small heatproof bowl and stand it in a larger heatproof bowl of boiling water. Let melt.

Put the nuts, dried apricots, squash, and ginger in a food processor and process until finely chopped. Add the melted coconut oil and coconut palm sugar and process again until the mixture starts to cling together. Spoon into the prepared pan sections and press down firmly. Chill.

Meanwhile, make the topping. Melt the coconut oil as above. Put the fresh apricots in a food processor and process to a puree. Scrape the thick layer of creamy milk from the top of the coconut milk into a bowl. (Reserve the liquid left in the can for another recipe.) Beat the creamy milk until peaking. Stir in the apricot puree and melted coconut oil and let stand for about 1 hour until thickened.

Lift the cakes out of the pan and transfer to a serving plate. Spoon or pipe on the apricot topping, then gently press whole almonds on top to decorate. Serve drizzled with maple syrup, if liked.

clementine & apple
TARTLETS

MAKES 12 • PREP TIME 20 minutes

4 clementines

Generous ¾ cup (150 g) dried currants

⅓ cup (50 g) sunflower seeds

Generous ⅓ cup (50 g) shelled pistachios, plus extra to decorate

2 tablespoons poppy seeds

2 dessert apples, quartered, cored, and grated

¼ teaspoon ground allspice

Place a large sheet of plastic wrap over a 12-section cupcake pan, then press into the sections to line them.

Finely grate the zest of 2 of the clementines. Put the currants, sunflower seeds, pistachios, and poppy seeds in a food processor with the clementine zest and process until the ingredients are very finely chopped and start to cling together. Place heaping dessertspoonfuls of the mixture in the prepared pan sections and press down firmly, using the back of a spoon or your fingers to make a dip in the centers. Chill until ready to serve.

Peel the clementines and chop the flesh. Combine together the apples, clementine flesh, and allspice, then tip into a food processor. Pulse very briefly to lightly break up the fruits. (Avoid over-processing or the fruit will turn to a thin puree.)

Transfer the cupcake shells to a serving plate. Spoon the fruit mixture on top and serve decorated with pistachios. (If liked, first steep the pistachios in boiling water for 1 minute, then drain and peel away the brown skins to reveal the emerald green nuts.)

PEACH & COCONUT CREAM CAKES

MAKES 4 • PREP TIME 20 minutes plus overnight chilling, soaking and freezing

¾ cup (100 g) cashews

½ cup (100 g) coarsely chopped dried peaches

Scant 1 cup (200 ml) coconut water

1 vanilla bean, chopped into small pieces

3 tablespoons agave nectar

1 (5½ oz/160 g) can coconut cream, chilled overnight

2 fresh peaches, halved, pitted, and thinly sliced

2 teaspoons lime juice

4 blackberries

Put the cashews in a bowl, cover with cold water and let soak for several hours or overnight. Put the dried peaches and coconut water in a separate bowl and let stand for 2 hours.

Place 4 x 2¾ inch (7 cm) baking rings on a small tray and line each with plastic wrap. Thoroughly drain the nuts, then transfer to a food processor. Add the dried peaches, coconut water, vanilla bean, and agave nectar and process to a smooth puree, scraping down the mixture from the sides of the bowl.

Beat the coconut cream in a bowl until slightly thickened. Scrape the peach mixture into the bowl and stir gently to combine. Divide among the baking rings.

Toss the peach slices with the lime juice in a small bowl. Arrange overlapping circles of the slices over the filling, working from the outer edges inwards and keeping the slices upright with the skin sides face up. The decoration should look a little like a rose when finished.

Freeze for at least 2 hours or overnight. Lift away the baking rings and remove the plastic wrap. Transfer the cakes to serving plates and place in the refrigerator for at least 4 hours before serving if frozen overnight. Top each with a blackberry to serve.

RAW BANOFFI PIE

SERVES 8 • PREP TIME 25 minutes plus overnight chilling and soaking

Scant ½ cup (75 g) Brazil nuts

½ cup (75 g) almonds

4 tablespoons hemp seeds

1¾ cups (300 g) pitted dates

½ cup (125 ml) coconut water

2 teaspoons vanilla extract

1 tablespoon maple syrup

3 large or 4 medium bananas

1 tablespoon lemon juice

2 (5½ oz/160 g) cans coconut cream, chilled overnight

2 tablespoons agave nectar

Sea salt

Put all the nuts in a bowl, cover with cold water and let soak for several hours or overnight. Thoroughly drain the nuts, then transfer to a food processor. Add the hemp seeds and process until finely ground. Add a generous ½ cup (100 g) of the dates and a pinch of salt and process again until the mixture starts to cling together. Tip into an 8¼–8½ inch (21–22 cm) loose-bottom flan pan. Using the back of a spoon, press the mixture firmly up the sides and into the bottom of the pan. Chill.

Meanwhile, put the remaining dates in a blender with the coconut water, vanilla extract, and a pinch of salt and blend to a thick, smooth paste. Press 2 tablespoons of the paste through a strainer to extract as much pulp as possible, scraping the mixture from the bottom of the strainer, then mix with the maple syrup to make a puree. Set aside the paste and the puree.

Slice the bananas and toss with the lemon juice. Arrange two-thirds over the crust and spread with the date paste.

Scrape off the thick layer of coconut cream into a bowl. Discard 1 tablespoon of the water left in each can, then add the remaining water to the bowl. Beat until thickened and softly peaking. Beat in the agave nectar, then spread over the filling. Scatter with the remaining bananas and drizzle with the reserved date puree. Chill until ready to serve.

chocolate walnut
FUDGE CAKE WITH MAPLE FROSTING

SERVES 12 • PREP TIME 20 minutes

1 cup (100 g) walnuts

1⅓ cups (200 g) almonds

1¾ oz (50 g) cacao butter (see page 5)

1 vanilla bean, chopped into pieces

¾ cup (150 g) dried figs

Generous ¼ cup (50 g) raisins

⅓ cup (40 g) cacao powder

5 tablespoons maple syrup

FOR THE FROSTING:

Generous 1 cup (150 g) cashews, coarsely chopped

3 tablespoons almond milk

⅓ cup (75 ml) maple syrup

¼ cup (25 g) cacao powder, plus extra for dusting

Put the walnuts, almonds, and cashews in separate bowls, cover with cold water and let soak for several hours or overnight. Put the cacao butter in a small heatproof bowl and stand it in a larger heatproof bowl of boiling water. Let melt.

Line a 6 inch (15 cm) round cake pan with plastic wrap. Thoroughly drain all the nuts, keeping them separate. Pulse the walnuts in a food processor until chopped, then tip out into a bowl and set aside.

Put the almonds and vanilla bean in the processor and process until finely ground. Add the melted cacao butter, figs, raisins, cacao powder, and maple syrup and mix to a thick paste. Remove the blade and stir in the reserved walnuts by hand. Turn the mixture into the prepared pan and press down firmly. Chill for at least 1 hour to firm up.

For the frosting, tip the cashews into the food processor and add the almond milk, maple syrup, and cacao powder. Process until thick and smooth, scraping down the mixture from the sides of the bowl.

Transfer the cake to a plate and peel away the plastic wrap. Spread the frosting over the top and sides with a metal spatula, keeping the surface as smooth as possible. Dust with cacao powder, to serve. If liked, use a ready-made stencil for a more decorative finish.

plum & oatmeal
UPSIDE-DOWN CAKE

SERVES 10 • PREP TIME 20 minutes plus chilling and soaking

1⅓ cups (200 g) almonds

6 plums, halved and pitted

1½ inch (4 cm) piece of fresh ginger root, grated

4 tablespoons almond milk

½ cup (125 ml) maple syrup, plus extra to serve (optional)

1 cup (150 g) medium oatmeal

Generous ½ cup (100 g) golden raisins

Put the almonds in a bowl, cover with cold water and let soak for several hours or overnight.

Line a 7 inch (18 cm) round cake pan with plastic wrap. Thoroughly drain the nuts, then put one in each of the cavities of 10 plum halves. Transfer to the prepared pan, cut sides down. Finely chop the remaining plum halves.

Combine the ginger, milk, and maple syrup in a small bowl. Put the remaining almonds in a food processor and process until finely ground. Add the oatmeal and golden raisins and process until the raisins are chopped. Add the milk mixture and blend to a paste. Remove the blade and stir in the chopped plums by hand.

Turn the mixture into the prepared pan and press down firmly to fill the gaps between the plums. Level the surface and chill for several hours or overnight.

To serve, invert the cake onto a serving plate and lift away the pan and plastic wrap. Cut into wedges with a sharp knife, preferably serrated. Serve drizzled with extra maple syrup, if liked.

mango & pistachio
CHOCOLATE FRIDGE CAKE

SERVES 8 • PREP TIME 10 minutes, plus soaking and chilling

Generous ½ cup (75 g) shelled pistachios

½ cup (75 g) almonds

2¾ oz (75 g) coconut oil

1½ cups (150 g) soft dried mango slices

⅔ cup (75 g) cacao powder

Good pinch of sea salt

Scant ½ cup (100 ml) agave nectar

1 tablespoon almond butter

Put all the nuts in a bowl, cover with cold water and let soak for several hours or overnight. Drain thoroughly and pat dry with paper towels.

Line a small 2½ cup (600 ml) loaf pan or similar-size container with plastic wrap or parchment paper.

Put the coconut oil in a small heatproof bowl and stand it in a larger heatproof bowl of boiling water. Let melt.

Combine the mango, nuts, cacao powder, and salt in a separate bowl. Drizzle with the agave nectar and mix together.

Stir the almond butter into the melted coconut oil, then drizzle over the cacao mixture. Stir well until thoroughly combined.

Turn the mixture into the prepared pan and press down firmly. Tap the pan on the counter to eliminate any pockets of air and chill for several hours until firm.

Turn out onto a board and peel away the plastic wrap or paper. Serve cut into slices.

chocolate mud pie

SERVES 8-10 • **PREP TIME** 20 minutes plus chilling and soaking

Scant 1½ cups (200 g) cashews

1 cup (150 g) hazelnuts

1¼ cups (225 g) plump dried apricots

1 teaspoon ground cinnamon

1¾ oz (50 g) cacao butter (see page 5)

Scant 1 cup (200 ml) almond milk

1 vanilla bean, chopped into small pieces

Scant ½ cup (50 g) cacao powder,
    plus 1 tablespoon

Scant ½ cup (100 ml) agave nectar,
    plus 3 tablespoons

Put the cashews and hazelnuts in separate bowls, cover with cold water and let soak for several hours or overnight.

Thoroughly drain the nuts, keeping them separate. Transfer a generous ¾ cup (125 g) of the hazelnuts to a food processor and process until chopped. Add a generous ¾ cup (150 g) of the apricots and the cinnamon and process again until the mixture starts to stick together. Tip into an 8 inch (20 cm) loose-bottom flan pan. Using the back of a spoon, press the mixture firmly up the sides and into the bottom of the pan. Chill.

Meanwhile, put the cacao butter in a small heatproof bowl and stand it in a larger heatproof bowl of boiling water. Let melt. Put the cashews, almond milk, vanilla bean, the scant ½ cup (50 g) cacao powder, and the scant ½ cup (100 ml) agave nectar in a food processor and process until completely smooth, scraping down the mixture from the sides of the bowl. Add the melted cacao butter and process to combine. Turn onto the crust and spread level. Freeze for 30 minutes or chill for 2–3 hours until firm.

Chop the remaining hazelnuts and apricots and scatter over the pie. Blend together the remaining cacao powder and agave nectar to make a smooth syrup. Transfer the pie to a plate and drizzle with the syrup to serve.

tangy lime & avocado
PLATE PIE

SERVES 8 • PREP TIME 20 minutes plus chilling and soaking

½ cup (75 g) almonds

Scant ½ cup (25 g) coconut chips

Generous ¾ cup (125 g) dried pears

2¾ oz (75 g) coconut oil

3 large ripe avocados

Finely grated zest of 3 limes, plus
   4 tablespoons juice

Scant ½ cup (100 ml) agave nectar

TO DECORATE:

2 limes

Small handful of coconut chips

1 tablespoon agave nectar

Put the almonds in a bowl, cover with cold water and let soak for several hours or overnight.

Thoroughly drain the nuts, then transfer to a food processor, add the coconut chips and process until chopped. Add the pears and process again until the mixture starts to stick together. Tip into an 8 inch (20 cm) pie plate. Using the back of a spoon, press the mixture down as firmly as you can. Chill.

Meanwhile, put the coconut oil in a small heatproof bowl and stand it in a larger heatproof bowl of boiling water. Let melt.

Halve and pit the avocados, then scoop the flesh into a blender. Add the lime zest, juice, and agave nectar and blend until smooth, scraping down the mixture from the sides of the bowl. Add the melted coconut oil and blend to mix. Turn out onto the crust and spread in an even layer. Chill for at least 3 hours or overnight until firm.

To decorate, cut away the zest from the limes. Working over a bowl to catch the juices, cut between the membranes to remove the segments. Scatter the segments and coconut chips over the middle of the pie. Mix the agave nectar with any juices collected in the bowl and spoon over the pie to serve.

MINTED PEAR & PECAN CAKE

SERVES 8 • PREP TIME 30 minutes, plus soaking and chilling

1¾ cups (175 g) pecans

4 small ripe pears

2 tablespoons lemon juice

1¾ oz (50 g) coconut oil

Generous ⅓ cup (50 g) cacao nibs

2¾ oz (75 g) coconut flesh

3 tablespoons coarsely chopped mint

Generous ¼ cup (50 g) raisins

3 tablespoons coconut blossom nectar

TO DECORATE:

3 tablespoons finely chopped pistachios

Mint sprigs

Put the pecans in a bowl, cover with cold water and let soak for several hours or overnight.

Dampen a 6 inch (15 cm) cake pan and line with plastic wrap. Quarter and core 2 of the pears and slice as thinly as possible. (The thinner the slices the easier they'll be to arrange and will look more impressive.) Put the slices in a bowl, toss with 1 tablespoon of the lemon juice and set aside.

Put the coconut oil in a small heatproof bowl and stand it in a larger heatproof bowl of boiling water. Let melt.

Thoroughly drain the nuts, then transfer to a food processor, add the cacao nibs, coconut flesh, and mint and process until finely chopped. Add the melted coconut oil, raisins, coconut blossom nectar, and remaining lemon juice and process until

the ingredients are thoroughly combined. Core and coarsely grate the remaining pears. Remove the blade from the processor bowl and stir in the grated pears.

Arrange overlapping slices of the reserved pear around the edges of the prepared pan and then in a circle in the bottom of the pan. (The slices need to be arranged so the outer edges of the pears show when the cake is turned out.) Carefully spoon the cake mixture into the pan, taking care not to dislodge the pear slices. Press down firmly and chill for at least 2 hours.

To serve, cut off any pear slices that are visible around the top edge of the cake. Invert the cake onto a plate and lift away the pan and plastic wrap. Sprinkle the pistachios around the top edge of the cake and decorate with sprigs of mint.

cherry & almond cake
WITH CHOCOLATE GANACHE

SERVES 10 • PREP TIME 25 minutes, plus soaking and chilling

1⅓ cups (200 g) almonds

1¾ oz (50 g) cacao butter (see page 5)

1 teaspoon almond extract

Generous ½ cup (75 g) coconut flour

3 tablespoons coconut palm sugar

2 cups (300 g) fresh cherries, pitted
and chopped, plus extra to decorate

FOR THE GANACHE:

8 oz (225 g) coconut oil

1½ cups (175 g) cacao powder

Scant 1 cup (225 ml) agave nectar

Put the almonds in a bowl, cover with cold water and let soak for several hours or overnight.

Line 2 x 6 inch (15 cm) round cake pans with plastic wrap.

To make the ganache, put the coconut oil in a small heatproof bowl and stand it in a larger heatproof bowl of boiling water. Let melt. Pour into a food processor, add the cacao powder and agave nectar and process until thick and glossy. Transfer to a clean heatproof bowl and set aside.

Put the cacao butter in a small heatproof bowl and stand it in a larger heatproof bowl of boiling water. Let melt.

Thoroughly drain the nuts, then transfer to the food processor

(there's no need to clean it). Add 4 tablespoons of the chocolate ganache, the almond extract, coconut flour, coconut palm sugar, and melted cacao butter. Process until combined. Remove the blade from the processor and stir in the chopped cherries. Divide between the prepared pans and press down firmly. Chill for at least 3 hours.

Carefully turn one of the cakes out onto a flat serving plate and peel away the plastic wrap. Spread with a third of the ganache mixture. (If the ganache has solidified, stand the bowl in a larger heatproof bowl of boiling water and leave until softened, stirring frequently.) Position the second cake on top and spread the top and sides with the remaining ganache. Serve decorated with extra cherries.

carrot cake
WITH LIME CASHEW FROSTING

SERVES 10 • PREP TIME 20 minutes plus chilling and soaking

7 carrots, about 1 lb 1 oz (525 g) total weight

1 cup (100 g) soft dried pineapple

1 teaspoon ground ginger

¼ teaspoon ground allspice

¾ cup (150 g) dried figs, stalks removed

Scant ½ cup (75 g) golden raisins

1 cup (150 g) medium oatmeal

Edible flowers, to decorate (optional)

FOR THE FROSTING:

Generous 1 cup (150 g) cashews

⅓ cup (75 ml) almond milk

Scant ¼ cup (50 ml) maple syrup

Finely grated zest of 1 lime, plus 3 teaspoons juice

Put the cashews in a bowl, cover with cold water and let soak for several hours or overnight.

Line 2 x 6 inch (15 cm) round cake pans with plastic wrap. Finely grate the carrots and pat dry between several thicknesses of paper towels.

Put the pineapple and spices in a food processor and process until chopped. Add the figs and process again until the mixture starts to cling together. Tip in the carrots, raisins, and oatmeal and process until evenly combined. Divide between the prepared pans and press down firmly.

Chill for several hours or freeze for 30 minutes to firm up.

To make the frosting, thoroughly drain the nuts, then transfer to a food processor, add the almond milk and process until smooth. Add the maple syrup, lime zest, and juice and thoroughly process until very thick, spreadable, and smooth, frequently scraping down the mixture from the sides of the bowl.

Carefully turn one of the carrot cakes out onto a flat serving plate and peel away the plastic wrap. Spread with half the frosting and top with the second cake. Spread with the remaining frosting and chill until ready to serve. Serve scattered with edible flowers, if liked.

COCONUT NEAPOLITAN CAKE

SERVES 8 • PREP TIME 45 minutes, plus soaking and chilling

1 cup (150 g) almonds

⅔ cup (100 g) hazelnuts

Generous ½ cup (100 g) Brazil nuts

8 oz (225 g) coconut flesh, brown skin removed

2½ oz (65 g) coconut oil

2½ tablespoons coconut palm sugar, plus 2 teaspoons

2 tablespoons cacao powder

1 teaspoon vanilla extract

⅓ cup (40 g) finely grated beet

Whipped Coconut Cream (see page 7), to serve

Put the almonds, hazelnuts, and Brazil nuts in separate bowls, cover with cold water and let soak for several hours or overnight.

Line a 4 inch (10 cm) round cake pan with plastic wrap. (Use a larger pan if you don't have a small one, though the cake will be very shallow.)

Put the coconut flesh in a food processor and process until finely ground. Remove 7 tablespoons and reserve for decoration.

Put the coconut oil in a small heatproof bowl and stand it in a larger heatproof bowl of boiling water. Let melt.

Drain the almonds, then put in a heatproof bowl and cover with very hot water. Let stand for 2 minutes, then drain and plunge into cold water for 1 minute to loosen the skins. Peel away the skins. (This takes a while and you don't need to be too thorough. Peeling them gives a better color to the finished cake, particularly the vanilla layer. Omit this step if you prefer.)

Drain the hazelnuts and Brazil nuts, then transfer to the food processor, add the almonds and the 2½ tablespoons coconut palm sugar and process until finely ground. Add the melted coconut oil and pulse briefly.

Put a third of the mixture in a separate bowl and beat in the cacao powder and remaining coconut palm sugar, then turn into the prepared pan and press down firmly. Beat the vanilla into half the remaining mixture, then pack into the pan on top of the chocolate mixture. Beat the beet into the remaining mixture and press into the pan. Freeze for 30 minutes to firm up slightly.

Put the reserved ground coconut on a plate. Carefully turn out the cake and remove the plastic wrap. Coat the sides and top of the cake in the coconut. Freeze for 30 minutes or chill for 1–2 hours to firm up a little.

Serve the cake cut into wedges with Whipped Coconut Cream.

SUMMER FRUITS CAKE

SERVES 6 • PREP TIME 20 minutes, plus overnight chilling and soaking

⅓ cup (50 g) almonds

Generous ½ cup (100 g) pitted dates

Small handful of basil leaves, plus extra
    to decorate

1 mini watermelon, about 3 lb 5 oz
    (1.5 kg)

1⅓ cups (200 g) strawberries, hulled and
    thinly sliced, plus extra to decorate

1 (5½ oz/160 g) can coconut cream,
    chilled overnight

1 tablespoon coconut blossom nectar

Put the almonds in a bowl, cover with cold water and let soak for several hours or overnight.

Line a 4 inch (10 cm) round cake pan with plastic wrap. (You can use a larger pan, but the cake will be more shallow.)

Thoroughly drain the nuts, then transfer to a food processor. Add the dates and process until the mixture is finely chopped and starts to cling together. Add the basil and pulse to combine.

Cut away the skin from the watermelon, keeping the fruit whole if possible, and cut into 6 x 4 inch (10 cm) slices, each about ¼ inch (5 mm) thick. (Reserve the rest of the fruit for another recipe.) Place one piece of the fruit in the bottom of the prepared pan. Add a layer of strawberry slices, then another slice of watermelon. Spoon half the date mixture on top and press down gently. Repeat the layering, finishing with a layer of watermelon. Chill for at least 1 hour.

Put the coconut cream and coconut blossom nectar in a bowl and beat until thickened. Invert the cake onto a plate and lift away the pan and plastic wrap. Decorate with extra strawberries and basil leaves, then cut into wedges and serve with the coconut cream.

raspberry, pistachio,
& ROSE SEMIFREDDO

MAKES 6 • PREP TIME 10 minutes plus overnight soaking, chilling, and freezing

Generous ½ cup (75 g) shelled pistachios

Generous 1 cup (150 g) raspberries,
plus extra to serve

2 (5½ oz/160 g) cans coconut cream,
chilled overnight

3 tablespoons agave nectar

1 teaspoon rose extract

Put the pistachios in a bowl, cover with cold water and let soak for several hours or overnight.

Line a small 2½ cup (600 ml) loaf pan or similar-size freezerproof container with plastic wrap.

Coarsely mash the raspberries with a fork. Drain the nuts, then coarsely chop.

Scrape off the thick layer of coconut cream into a bowl. Discard 1 tablespoon of the water left in each can, then add the remaining water to the bowl. Beat until thickened and softly peaking. Beat in the agave nectar and rose extract.

Gently stir in the pistachios and raspberries and tip the mixture into the prepared pan. Spread the surface level and freeze for at least 4 hours or overnight until firmed up.

If frozen overnight, transfer the semifreddo to the refrigerator about 1 hour before serving. Invert onto a plate or board and peel away the plastic wrap. Cut into slices and serve scattered with extra raspberries.

blackberry & star anise
FREEZER CAKE

SERVES 10 • PREP TIME 20 minutes plus overnight soaking and freezing

Scant 1½ cups (200 g) cashews

8 whole star anise or 4 teaspoons ground anise, plus 1 whole star anise to decorate

1½ cups (350 ml) almond milk or oat milk

Scant ½ cup (100 ml) agave nectar

1¾ cups (250 g) blackberries

1 tablespoon lime juice

TO SERVE:

½ cup (75 g) dried pears, coarsely chopped

2 tablespoons pumpkin seeds

¾ cup (100 g) blackberries

Put the cashews in a bowl, cover with cold water and let soak overnight.

Line a 6 inch (15 cm) round cake pan with plastic wrap. If using whole star anise, grind to a powder in a small food grinder or processor.

Drain the nuts, then transfer to a food processor, add the almond or oat milk and process until smooth, scraping down the mixture from the sides of the bowl. Add the star anise powder, agave nectar, blackberries, and lime juice and process until completely smooth.

Press the mixture through a strainer into a bowl, then transfer to the prepared pan. Freeze for at least 4 hours or overnight until firm.

To make the topping, put the pears and pumpkin seeds in the food processor and process until chopped.

To serve, transfer the cake to a serving plate and let soften in the refrigerator for about 1 hour. Scatter with the pears, pumpkin seeds, and blackberries. Decorate with the whole star anise.

blueberry
& VANILLA CAKE

SERVES 12 • PREP TIME 20 minutes plus soaking and freezing

⅔ cup (100 g) almonds

Scant 2¼ cups (300 g) cashews

4 tablespoons sunflower seeds

Generous ¾ cup (150 g) pitted dates

Generous 1 cup (150 g) fresh blueberries, plus extra to decorate

⅓ cup (50 g) dried blueberries

2¾ oz (75 g) coconut oil

2 vanilla beans, chopped into small pieces

1½ cups (350 ml) almond milk

Scant ½ cup (100 ml) agave nectar

2 teaspoons apple cider vinegar

Mint or lemon balm leaves, to decorate

Put the almonds and cashews in separate bowls, cover with cold water and let soak for several hours or overnight.

Thoroughly drain the almonds, then transfer to a food processor and process until chopped. Add the sunflower seeds and dates and process again until the mixture is finely ground and starts to cling together. Turn into a 7 inch (18 cm) loose-bottom cake pan and press down firmly.

Wipe out the food processor, add the fresh and dried blueberries, and pulse briefly until mashed. Tip onto the almond crust and spread in an even layer, pressing down gently. Chill.

Put the coconut oil in a small heatproof bowl and stand it in a larger heatproof bowl of boiling water. Let melt.

Drain the cashews, then transfer to a food processor, add the vanilla beans, almond milk, agave nectar, and cider vinegar and process until smooth, scraping down the mixture from the sides of the bowl. Add the melted coconut oil and blend until evenly combined. Spoon over the blueberry filling, then freeze for at least 6 hours or overnight.

To serve, transfer the cake to a serving plate and let soften in the refrigerator for about 1 hour. Serve scattered with extra blueberries and mint or lemon balm leaves.

strawberry & vanilla
CHEESECAKE

SERVES 8–10 • **PREP TIME** 25 minutes, plus soaking and chilling

Scant 1 cup (125 g) almonds

Scant 2¼ cups (300 g) cashews

Generous ¾ cup (150 g) pitted dates

3 tablespoons coconut flour

2¾ oz (75 g) coconut oil

1 vanilla bean

1¼ cups (300 ml) coconut water

⅓ cup (75 ml) agave nectar

1 tablespoon lemon juice

Scant 2¼ cups (300 g) strawberries, hulled and thinly sliced, plus extra to serve

Put the almonds and cashews in separate bowls, cover with cold water and let soak for several hours or overnight.

Thoroughly drain the almonds, then transfer to a food processor and process until finely chopped. Add the dates and coconut flour and process again until it is the consistency of fine ground cookies and starts to cling together. Using the back of a spoon, press the mixture firmly up the sides slightly and into the bottom of an 8 inch (20 cm) loose-bottom cake pan. Chill. Meanwhile, put the coconut oil in a small heatproof bowl and stand it in a larger heatproof bowl of boiling water. Let melt.

Thoroughly drain the cashews. Split the vanilla bean open and scrape out the seeds with the tip of a knife. Put the vanilla seeds in a food processor with the cashews and coconut water and process until smooth, scraping down the mixture from the sides of the bowl. Add the melted coconut oil, agave nectar, and lemon juice and process again until pale and smooth.

Arrange half the strawberries over the almond crust. Spoon half the cashew filling on top and spread level. Scatter over the remaining strawberries, then top with the remaining filling and spread level. Freeze for 3–4 hours to firm up.

Loosen the edges of the cheesecake and remove from the pan. Transfer to a serving plate while still semi-frozen and let soften in the refrigerator for a couple of hours or until ready to serve. Serve decorated with extra strawberries.

banana & date
RIPPLE ICE CREAM CAKE

SERVES 10 • PREP TIME 15 minutes plus freezing

9 ripe bananas

Scant 1½ cups (250 g) pitted dates

½ teaspoon sea salt

Scant ½ cup (100 ml) water

Squeeze of lemon or lime juice

TO SERVE:

2 small bananas

2 teaspoons lemon juice

Generous ¼ cup (50 g) pitted dates, chopped

¼ cup (25 g) sliced almonds

Freeze the 9 bananas in their skins for at least 6 hours or overnight.

Line a 7 inch (18 cm) round cake pan with plastic wrap.

Put the dates in a food processor and process until finely chopped. Add the salt and measurement water and blend to a smooth paste, scraping down the mixture from the sides of the bowl. Transfer to a bowl and rinse out the food processor.

Slice the frozen bananas into the processor. (If the bananas have been frozen overnight, run them under warm water first so you can peel away the skins.) Add a squeeze of lemon or lime juice and process until pale and creamy, scraping down any pieces of banana from the sides of the bowl.

Spoon a quarter of the banana mixture into the prepared pan and spread level. Add a third of the date puree and spread to cover the bananas. Add another quarter of the bananas and half the remaining date puree. Repeat the layering, finishing with a layer of banana. Freeze for 4–6 hours or overnight until frozen.

To serve, transfer the ice cream cake to the refrigerator about 2 hours before serving. Remove from the pan, peel away the plastic wrap and transfer to a serving plate. Slice the bananas and toss with the lemon juice. Scatter over the ice cream cake with the dates and almonds and serve cut into thin wedges.

CHOCOLATE COCONUT BARS

MAKES 16 • PREP TIME 20 minutes, plus chilling and setting

1¾ oz (50 g) coconut oil

1 fresh coconut, about 1 lb 1 oz (500 g), or 9¾ oz (275 g) coconut flesh, coarsely chopped

1¾ oz (50 g) pack creamed coconut, chopped

2 tablespoons coconut blossom nectar

FOR THE COATING:

2¾ oz (75 g) cacao butter (see page 5)

⅔ cup (75 g) cacao powder

5 tablespoons coconut blossom nectar

Line a 7 inch (18 cm) square shallow baking pan with plastic wrap. Line a baking sheet with parchment paper. Put the coconut oil in a small heatproof bowl and stand it in a larger heatproof bowl of boiling water. Let melt.

Crack open the coconut, if using, remove the flesh and coarsely chop. Put the coconut flesh, creamed coconut, and coconut blossom nectar in a food processor and process until finely ground. Add the melted coconut oil and process until the mixture starts to cling together. Transfer to the prepared baking pan and press down firmly in an even layer. Chill for 1 hour or until firm.

To make the chocolate coating, put the cacao butter in a small heatproof bowl and stand it in a larger heatproof bowl of boiling water. Let melt. If the water cools before the cacao butter melts, replace with more boiled water.

Remove the coconut slab from the pan and cut in half, then cut each half into 8 bars.

Scrape the melted cacao butter into a larger, shallow bowl and stir in the cacao powder and coconut blossom nectar. Lower a coconut bar into the sauce and turn to coat. Lift out on a fork, letting the excess sauce drip back into the bowl, then transfer to the prepared baking sheet. Repeat with the remaining bars. Let set in a cool place or the refrigerator.

CHEWY BERRY BITES

MAKES 9 • PREP TIME 10 minutes plus standing

Generous ½ cup (100 g) pitted dates

½ cup (50 g) jumbo rolled oats

½ cup (75 g) dried blueberries

½ cup (75 g) dried cranberries

¼ cup (25 g) goji berries

4 tablespoons chia seeds

1 teaspoon apple cider vinegar

Line a 4½ inch (12 cm) square container with plastic wrap.

Put the dates and oats in a food processor and process to fine crumbs. Add the blueberries, cranberries, goji berries, chia seeds, and vinegar and process again until the mixture starts to clump together.

Turn into the prepared container and press down firmly in an even layer using your hands. Let stand for 2–3 hours to firm up slightly. Serve cut into 9 small squares.

CHOCOLATE ORANGE NUGGETS

MAKES about 9 oz (250 g) • **PREP TIME** 10 minutes plus soaking and standing

Generous ⅓ cup (60 g) almonds

Finely grated zest of 1 orange

1 cup (175 g) pitted dates

⅓ cup (40 g) cacao powder, plus extra
for dusting

½ teaspoon sea salt

Put the almonds in a bowl, cover
with cold water and let soak for
several hours or overnight.

Thoroughly drain the nuts, then
transfer to a food processor and
process until finely ground. Add
the orange zest, dates, cacao
powder, and salt and process
again until the mixture starts
to cling together.

Take teaspoonfuls of the mixture
and press together into irregular,
bite-size pieces. Dust with extra
cacao powder and let stand for
1 hour to firm up slightly.

peppery lime
CHOCOLATE BARS

MAKES 2 small bars • **PREP TIME** 10 minutes, plus chilling

Finely grated zest of 2 limes

¼ teaspoon cayenne pepper

3½ oz (100 g) cacao butter (see page 5)

⅓ cup (40 g) cacao powder

Scant ½ cup (50 ml) agave nectar

Line 2 small containers, each about 5 x 3½ inches (12 x 9 cm), with plastic wrap. (Small plastic sandwich boxes are ideal.)

Put the lime zest, cayenne pepper, and cacao butter in a heatproof bowl and stand it in a larger heatproof bowl of boiling water. Let melt, stirring frequently. If the water cools before the cacao melts, replace with more boiled water.

Lift the bowl out and beat in the cacao powder until the mixture is smooth and glossy. Stir in the agave nectar. Pour into the prepared containers and chill for about 1 hour until set. Peel away the plastic wrap and serve broken into pieces.

VARIATIONS: Add the finely grated zest of 1 orange, or ⅓ cup (50 g) chopped hazelnuts and scant ¼ cup (25 g) raisins, instead of the lime zest and cayenne.

ALMOND & WALNUT FUDGE

MAKES 14 oz (400 g) • **PREP TIME** 10 minutes, plus soaking and freezing

Generous ¾ cup (125 g) almonds

¾ cup (75 g) walnuts

1¾ oz (50 g) coconut oil

1 banana

1 teaspoon vanilla extract

2 tablespoons almond butter

3 tablespoons coconut blossom nectar

2 large pitted dates

Good pinch of sea salt

Put the almonds and walnuts in separate bowls, cover with cold water and let soak for several hours or overnight.

Put the coconut oil in a small heatproof bowl and stand it in a larger heatproof bowl of boiling water. Let melt.

Line a small container, about 6 inches (15 cm) square, with plastic wrap.

Thoroughly drain the nuts, keeping them separate. Chop the walnuts and set aside. Transfer the almonds to a food processor and process until finely ground. Chop the banana into the processor and add the melted coconut oil, vanilla extract, almond butter, coconut blossom nectar, dates, and salt. Process again to a thick paste. Remove the blade and stir in the walnuts by hand.

Turn the mixture into the prepared container, level the surface and press down firmly. Freeze for about 1 hour until firm. Serve cut into small squares.

INDEX

GLOSSARY

beet : beetroot
coconut chips : coconut flakes
cupcake cups : cupcake cases
crust : base (e.g., cheesecake base)
golden raisins : sultanas
metal spatula : palette knife
pan : tin
paper towel : kitchen paper
plastic wrap : cling film
pumpkin pie spice : ground mixed spice
rolled oats : porridge oats
shell : case
sliced almonds : flaked almonds
strainer : sieve
vanilla bean : vanilla pod
zest: rind

ACKNOWLEDGMENTS

CONSULTANT PUBLISHER: Sarah Ford
EDITOR: Alex Stetter
COPY EDITOR: Joanne Murray
DESIGNERS: Jaz Bahra and Eoghan O'Brien
PHOTOGRAPHER: Lis Parsons
FOOD STYLIST: Joanna Farrow
PROPS STYLIST: Liz Hippisley
PRODUCTION CONTROLLER: Meskerem Berhane